BEFORE THE ANASAZI
Early Man on the Colorado Plateau

by
Larry D. Agenbroad

Museum of Northern Arizona

"Mammoth Kill." Acrylic painting by Denny Carley

INTRODUCTION

Imagine, if you will, that you are a Paleo-Indian hunter 11,300 years ago, somewhere in the terrain that is now called the Colorado Plateau. You are one of a group of hunters—all extended family members. You have just heard a mammoth trumpet. After an interval of stalking through the spruce and birch trees near a stream, you have your first glimpse of the quarry. Silently, with hand signals, you and your group position yourselves downwind to move in for the kill. In a flurry of action, noise, and danger, several spears pierce the animal's vital organs. The huge creature is dead, and you begin the monumental task of skinning and butchering the carcass. Here is meat! *Tons* of meat, enough (with proper preparation and storage) to provide food for the entire band through much of the coming winter.

This scenario (or one like it) was carried out with some frequency on the Colorado Plateau. Just a bit later in time, it would have been a similar scene but with bison as the intended prey. While it is very difficult to establish the presence of Paleo-Indian hunters in such life-and-death situations on the Colorado Plateau, we can get some clues from the "other" (or pre-ceramic) archaeology.

Until just a few years ago, most archaeologists denied the presence of early man on the Colorado Plateau. New evidence, however, has forced a rethinking of this position. Results of research conducted over the past decade, for example, have provided us with new insight into important changes in plant and animal life over the past 11,000 years. It is part of a pattern that documents the Pleistocene presence of Paleo-Indian hunters of extinct, ice-age fauna, and their descendants, through at least 9,000 years of plateau prehistory *prior to* the Anasazi.

THE PLEISTOCENE ENVIRONMENT

Before we can understand how early man came to be on the Colorado Plateau or how he survived here, we must examine the physical conditions present in this area during the late Pleistocene. In fact, it is necessary to look at conditions even farther afield—the northern portions of North America and the northeastern corner of the Eurasian land mass. For it is from these regions that we think the earliest humans on the Colorado Plateau came. Who were these people? Where exactly did they come from? And how and when did they get here?

The most recent period of the earth's history, the Quaternary, is separated into two parts—the Pleistocene (which goes back nearly two million years) and the Holocene (the last 10,000 years). We often refer to the Pleistocene as the "Ice Age" because of repeated episodes of glacial activity throughout these years. The most recent period of glaciation in North America is known as the Wisconsin. The glacial advance began approximately 50,000 years ago, reached its maximum by 25,000 years ago, and was essentially over by 11,000 years ago. The Holocene (or Recent) is usually considered to cover the last 10,000 years.

Continental glaciations caused many physical changes on the planet. One such change during the Wisconsin glacial advance was a lowering of the eustatic (worldwide) sea level by as much as 300 feet because water was being lost from the ocean and being stored as ice and snow on the continental land masses. The glaciation provided much cooler and moister climatic conditions in many areas that now have temperate to desert environments. It also caused the modification, coverage, or isolation of large areas of continental land mass because glaciers and ice sheets formed. These factors also affected the plant and animal communities by eradicating some species or forcing others to move southward to warmer regions.

One of the most important events of the Pleistocene was the establishment of a land bridge (the Bering Land Bridge) that connected two hemispheres in the present location of the Bering Strait. It was a direct result of the "dewatering" of the ocean. As the water level dropped, a land connection between Siberia and Alaska, estimated to be as wide as 1200 miles in a north-south dimension, became available for use in two periods during the last glaciation: 15,000 to 24,000 years ago and 9,000 to 11,000 years ago. The importance of the Bering Land Bridge is that it served as a "drawbridge" allowing intercontinental migration of both plants and animals between the Old World and the New World. Some of the "travelers" on this bridge, during its existence, were camels and horses, who went from the New to the Old World (ultimately becoming extinct in the former while remaining as modern inhabitants of the latter).

4

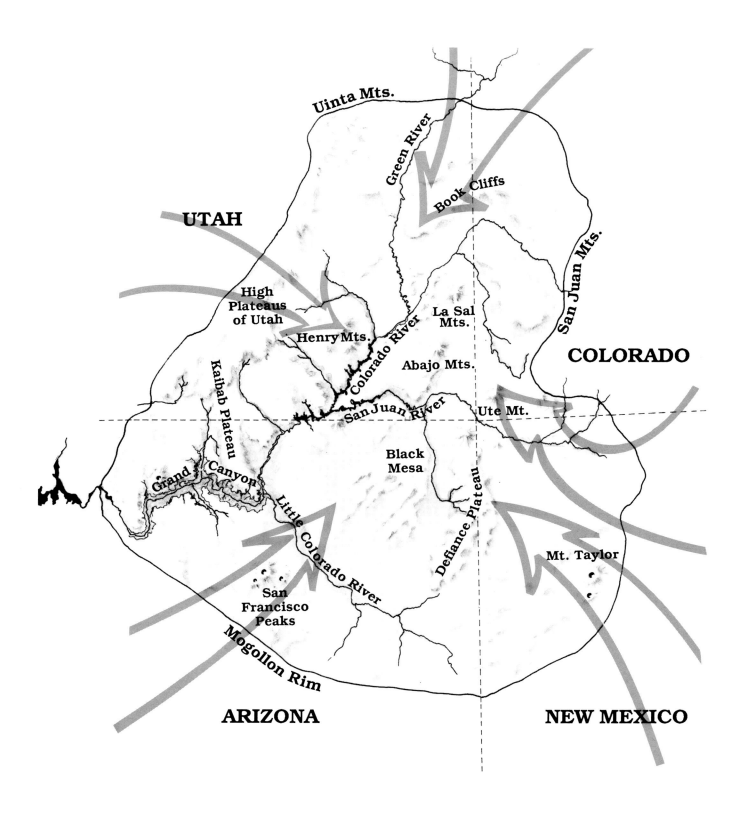

Map of the Colorado Plateau showing possible travel routes by Paleo-Indian and Archaic groups from the Great Basin, Rocky Mountains and High Plains, and the Desert Southwest.

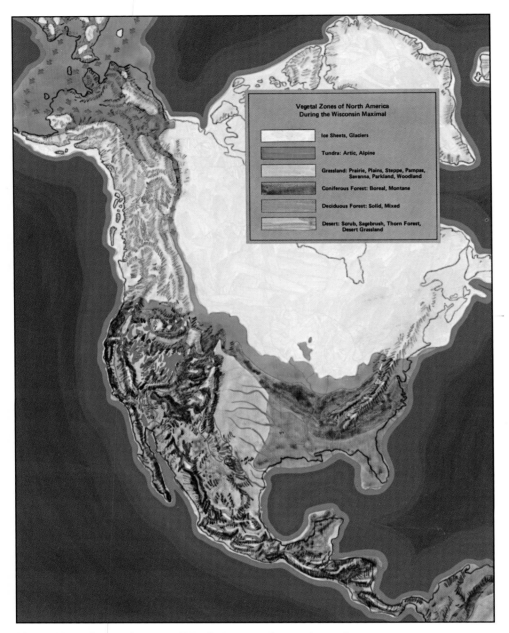

Vegetal Zones of North America
During the Wisconsin Maximal

Ice Sheets, Glaciers

Tundra: Artic, Alpine

Grassland: Prairie, Plains, Steppe, Pampas,
Savanna, Parkland, Woodland

Coniferous Forest: Boreal, Montane

Deciduous Forest: Solid, Mixed

Desert: Scrub, Sagebrush, Thorn Forest,
Desert Grassland

Above: Map of vegetal zones of North America during the peak
of the last ice age. Orange arrows show probable migratory routes.
Opposite right: "New World Antecedents from the Old World."
Acrylic paintings by Denny Carley

In the opposite direction, Old World forms such as the mastodons, mammoths, bison, shrub oxen, ursine bears, moose, rodents, and humans arrived in the New World. The new arrivals probably had no concept of having entered a new land mass. The peopling of the Americas may have been an accident caused by hunters and hunted being stranded on this new land mass by the rising sea level fed by meltwater from continental ice. This meltwater re-established the open sea we refer to as the Bering Strait.

The unglaciated drainage system of the Yukon River created a large sanctuary ("refugium") for these new arrivals. Once there, they were forced to stay since they were prevented from further travel by the coalescence of the Cordilleran (Rocky Mountain) ice cap and the

"Pleistocene Reconstruction." Painting by Nova Young.
Photograph by Marc Gaede, from the MNA photo archives

Laurentide ice sheet. These two incredibly large masses of ice flowed downward from their respective centers and either calved at sea or merged in west-central Canada and pushed southward into the prairie and plains of north-central North America. As the lowering of sea level created a "drawbridge" we referred to as the Bering Land Bridge, it also created a "tollgate" in west-central Canada—the closing of a travel path to temperate portions of the continent. These processes also may have happened in prior glaciations. Of importance to our discussion is the fact that humans were among the creatures to cross into the New World during the last period of glaciation.

There are two basic (and opposing) theories about when humans arrived in the New World. One suggests the presence of humans prior to 15,000 years ago. A second theory holds that human groups

8

Above: Presentday bison. Photograph by Larry Agenbroad
Right: "A Band of Nomadic Big-Game Hunters Entering the
New World during the Wisconsin Glaciation."
Acrylic painting by Denny Carley

post-date 15,000 years ago. There are a number of advocates for an "early-early" human presence in North America. The problem facing these proponents is to convince the majority of the professional community that their "sites" are truly human produced, not natural occurrences. Another problem is the current lack of evidence for the peopling of Siberia prior to 20,000 years ago. This, coupled with what we know about the periods in which the land bridge existed, limits the timing of human migration to the New World. It seems most likely that New World Paleo-Indians were of Siberian origin, entering the continent via the Bering Land Bridge some time after 20,000 years ago.

Although a few archaeologists have advanced claims regarding the discovery of cultural materials, butchering patterns, and bone and stone modification that pre-date 15,000 years ago, there are factors that prevent the universal acceptance of their sites. Three important problems with the sites examined so far are (1) they tend to be unique occurrences; (2) the chronological data used to date them is suspect for a variety of reasons; and (3) there is little indication of a moderately prolific human stock, i.e., no descendants. Thus, most early-early sites tend to fail the "tests" of replicability, valid chronology, and undeniable cultural association.

One theory of early-early migration holds that the people came south along the west coast of North America. In my opinion, the proponents of this theory have never tried to traverse the terminus of an active glacier. These early travelers would have to cross not just the impressive glacial termini of Alaska today, but the approximately 2,000 miles of glacial termini of the Wisconsin Ice. It is apparent that both hunters and hunted had to await the opening of the "tollgate"—the separation of the Cordilleran and Laurentide ice masses. This disjuncture would create an ice-free corridor just east of the Rocky Mountains, in the prairie provinces of southwestern and south-central Canada.

Packrat middens.
Photograph by Emilee Mead

It possibly would take less than 1,000 years for a small hunting group and their descendents to travel from the locality of presentday Edmonton, Alberta, to the more southerly latitudes of the Colorado Plateau. We know that Clovis people (described below) were present in Cochise County, in southeastern Arizona, by 11,300 years ago. There are several mammoth-kill sites on, or near, the San Pedro River that give us ample evidence of their success in killing, processing, and consuming mammoth and lesser animals.

What kind of environment would these "pioneers" encounter as they penetrated the physiographic province we call the Colorado Plateau? What was it like 11,000 years ago when Pleistocene man stalked now-extinct Pleistocene animals?

Any reconstruction of the paleo-environment of 11,000 years ago must rely on scientific "detective" work, often using clues that are invisible to the unaided eye. Such clues take the form of microscopic grains of pollen from plants in that environment, which provide information on the temperature and moisture of the area at a specific point in time. Additional clues are provided by the study of sediments. We can determine the manner in which these sediments were deposited (whether they are windblown or lake or stream deposited). These analyses help us to understand the amounts of moisture available as runoff. In the opposite sense, they can tell us of drought that allowed the wind to become a dominant transport and depositional agent. Still other clues are gathered from an examination of packrat middens. These rodents gather and store plant and animal remains both for food and for construction of their nests. Packrat middens dating back 11,000 years almost certainly would contain extinct or extralocal remains. Additional information comes from an analysis of modern environments in which those plants and animals still exist.

All of this allows a partial interpretation of the ancient environment. Fossil remains—including the hard parts (bones, teeth) as well as the soft parts (hair, hide, horns, claws, hooves, dung) of the fauna—give us clues as to who and what were living there. One incredibly valuable set of clues initially does not seem too appealing—dung. Because of the Colorado Plateau's arid nature, it is well suited to the preservation of dung. Analogous to, if not as glamorous as, mummified remains from Egypt, the dung is especially useful because it can be dated precisely; it can be tested to determine the botanical components, and it can be chemically identified to genus. A combination of these techniques provides quite an accurate reconstruction of the ancient environment.

For example, evidence from the central Colorado Plateau indicates that when the mammoths, shrub oxen, bison, sloths, camels, and horses went out to dine they consumed items such as tall grass, water plants, sagebrush, willows, rose, oak, birch, spruce, cacti, and other forage. Most of those dietary items no longer exist in the area where the dung has been preserved. One reconstructed plant community can be found in the region, but it is 4,000 feet higher in elevation than it was 11,000 years ago when it was "lunch" at the locality. The fact that the plants found in the dung are now surviving at a much higher elevation (or latitude) tells us it was much cooler and more moist at that locality 11,000 years ago. This provides us with evidence of rather severe environmental change in the past 11,000 years. If we find it hard to believe that what is now an arid shrub and scrub canyon was a riparian forest just 11,000 years ago, think what the modern environment would seem like to a Clovis hunter.

The human response to the challenge of a changing environment—of Pleistocene peoples adaptation to new environmental conditions—is where an important part of the mystery and intrigue of the Colorado Plateau's human prehistory lies.

A PHILOSOPHICAL AND HISTORICAL PERSPECTIVE

Several problems are inherent with a discussion of early human cultures on the Colorado Plateau. The foremost of these is the preoccupation of the vast majority of the archaeological community with Anasazi (ceramic) archaeology. Until recently, it was nearly impossible to date sites that did not contain pottery fragments. But with the advent of radiocarbon dating and other sophisticated techniques, researchers can now assign dates to these sites. Unfortunately, the tendency of archaeological researchers to treat earlier sites as nondiagnostic or insignificant did not disappear in response to new realities. Only in very recent (post-1970) intensive surveys requiring an examination of *all* cultural aspects of the survey areas has this bias been somewhat overcome.

A second problem is the focus of most survey efforts on the Colorado Plateau. Because of the way we fund archaeological studies, major archaeological activity has concentrated on areas of known prehistory, areas of energy resource exploitation, areas where surface modifications of one type or another are planned, and areas of heavy public use—such as national parks, proposed wilderness areas, and state parks. This bias means that research tools like distribution maps, which show specific sites for animal remains, Indian artifacts, etc., are not reliable. Until we have samples from a wider variety of sites, it is foolish to theorize the "presence" or "absence" of any cultural entities in the Southwest. I suspect that the distribution

General view of a Pleistocene cave excavated by Lyndon Hargrave at Camp Anasazee. Photograph by D. F. Walkington, from the MNA photo archives

Above: Mammoth ribs in alcove on the Colorado Plateau.
Right: Mammoth tusks on the Colorado River above Moab.
Photographs by Larry Agenbroad

maps presented in this *Plateau* would look very different if an "equal effort for equal area" approach was possible.

A third problem is one I will call "political." Political boundaries such as state and county boundaries, agency jurisdiction boundaries, and even philosophical boundaries result in different approaches to the investigation, analysis, and interpretation of an area's prehistory. One political entity may be interested in only one small aspect of a region's prehistory, ignoring all others, while another political entity may desire to investigate the entire spectrum of prehistory. One agency may be a prolific producer of syntheses and reports, whereas another entity may apply a "retrieve and store" philosophy to an adjacent area. With so many different approaches to the region's prehistory, archaeologists find it very difficult to synthesize information on the Colorado Plateau, which encompasses and crosscuts many of these "political" entities.

A final problem is that even with the increased evidence of relatively abundant Pleistocene fauna constituting a resource base, and the documented evidence of Clovis hunters on the Colorado Plateau, we still do not have a site with direct association of man and extinct fauna on the plateau. I feel it is only a matter of time until a locality with such direct association is found. The region is "pregnant" with the potential for such a discovery.

As we near the end of the twentieth century, some of these research problems appear solvable. We are learning better techniques for researching Pleistocene and Archaic sites. Changes in philosophy, funding, and dissemination of information also are improving the situation. As a result, the research bias toward ceramic sites is diminishing. But it will be some time before archaeologists are able to tell a more complete story about early human prehistory on the Colorado Plateau.

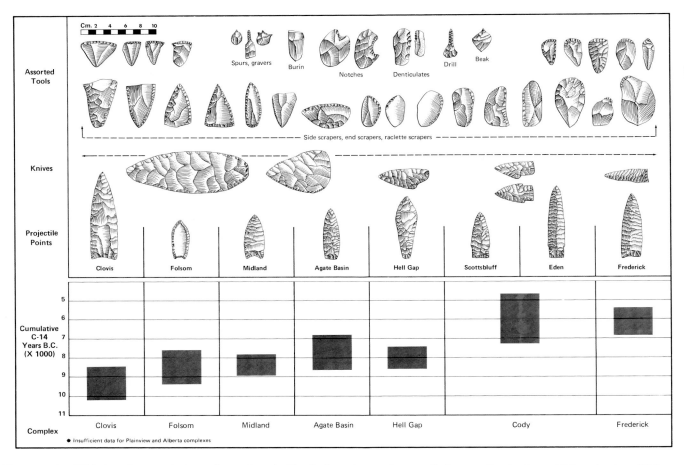

Comparative lithic typology and chronology of early North American cultures. Redrawn after Irwin and Wormington, 1970.

Paleo-Indians

The term "Paleo-Indian" came into use in the mid-twentieth century to identify what we might describe as the first Americans. The common usage of the term infers an antiquity of greater than 8,000 years, with the term "Archaic" referring to the culture from 8,000 years ago to the beginnings of settled agriculture and production of ceramics. "Formative" is the term archaeologists use to identify groups established approximately 2,000 years ago.

Five cultural stages have been proposed for North American prehistory. Only three of the cultural stages—the Lithic, Archaic, and Formative—occur north of Mexico. The term "Paleo-Indian" is somewhat synonymous with "lithic." Traditionally, the lithic is divided into two substages—Llano (older) and Plano (younger). The Llano often is further divided into Clovis (older) and Folsom (younger).

The earliest universally accepted cultural entity in the Southwest is the Clovis culture, which is considered to be older than 11,000 years. This is the first widespread, archaeologically visible cultural group in the New World. These people were specialized big-game hunters of Pleistocene animals, such as mammoth, but they also stalked smaller forms of extinct and modern fauna.

14

They were named for projectile points first recognized at Dent, Colorado, but found in abundance at Blackwater Draw, near Clovis, New Mexico. What we know of the Clovis culture has been gathered primarily from kill site associations of extinct fauna (mostly mammoth) and a diagnostic projectile point, the Clovis point.

The discovery of the Clovis point (and the earlier identification of what we now call the Folsom point) revolutionized our concepts of the antiquity of man in the New World. In the intervening 52 years, we have come to know more about Clovis distribution and specific sites, yet we are still perplexed as to the temporal and technological origin of these people, their lifeways, and their effects on the environment.

NORTH AMERICAN CULTURAL STAGES*

POST CLASSIC: approximately A.D. 1300 until after Spanish contact. Characterized by warfare and competition. Brought to a close by Cortez, Pizarro, etc.

CLASSIC: approximately A.D. 1000 to A.D. 1300. Rise of city states with political, religious, military, scientific, and commoner stratification. Storable surplus food, elaborate religious structures, observatories.

FORMATIVE: approximately 1,000 to 2,000 years ago. Beginning agriculture, first as horticulture, advancing to sedentary lifestyle with simple village structure. Social system evolution and more formalized religious structures (kivas).

ARCHAIC: approximately 2,000 to 6,000 years ago. Increased dependence on plant resources. Semi-sedentary settlement pattern. Seasonal exploitation of plant resources, beginning experimentation with planting. Abundant evidence of plant food processing artifacts such as manos and metates.

LITHIC: approximately 6,000 to 15,000 years ago. Two substages:

PLANO: specialized bison hunters with a variety of projectile point styles. Most are associated with extinct forms of bison. Lanceolate projectile points of stemmed and shouldered styles.

LLANO: 10,000 to 15,000 before present. Two divisions:

FOLSOM: approximately 6,000 years ago. Lanceolate, fluted projectile points with extinct bison.

CLOVIS: older than 11,000 years ago. Large projectile points. Mammoth and extinct bison. Specialized big-game hunters. First archaeologically visible cultural group in the New World.

*Willey and Phillips, *Methodology and Theory in American Archaeology* (Chicago: University of Chicago Press), 1958.

Opposite, top: Clovis and Folsom projectile points
Opposite, bottom: Plano projectile points
Above: Archaic projectile points
Photographs by Denny Carley

EARLY PALEO-INDIAN CULTURES

The Clovis

The Clovis culture is defined by the presence of distinctive lanceolate, fluted points associated in kill sites with extinct and modern prey animals. Only a few camp sites are know to offer additional data. Much of what is known about the geographical distribution of Clovis is available only from surface finds of isolated points or their variants. It has been stated that "...the Clovis industry is [the first] continent-wide complex," referring to North America.

Clovis Origins

Geographically, people of the Clovis culture originated from Siberian stock, crossed the Bering Strait, and migrated to southern North America, where their culture became widespread and archaeologically visible. Three possible origins for Clovis people have been proposed: 1) an independent origin in several regions; 2) development in the American High Plains with subsequent dispersal throughout the New World; or, 3) development in Alaska with a subsequent southern migration.

If Clovis is the first widespread, archaeologically visible lithic (or stone-artifact based) culture in the southern portion of North America that is compatible with what is known about the dating of the initial occupation of the Western Hemisphere, its origins must ultimately be derived from a more northern culture. Today, we are fairly certain that Clovis were one subset of the peoples who crossed into the New World across the Bering Strait. Recently, some archaeologists have suggested that Clovis is derived from the Alaskan Nenana Complex, after the people of that cultural complex were south of the ice-free corridor.

Clovis Lifeways

The Clovis usually formed fairly small cultural units, probably less than forty persons, including both sexes and all ages. They were specialized megafauna (or big-game) hunters, taking mammoths and, less frequently, bison and smaller game. Some sites, such as Kimmswick (Missouri), Manis (Washington), and perhaps Lake Pleasant (Michigan), suggest possible mastodon (*Mammut americanum*) procurement as well.

Clovis kill and camp sites were located at or near water sources such as springs or small streams—an indication that the animals usually were ambushed at or near water. It may be that the groundwater tables were dropping and that surface moisture was less abundant during Clovis time. It appears that this continued into the Holocene, at least until the altithermal drought (a drought character-

18

ized by rising temperatures) four thousand to seven thousand years ago. Although some researchers believe that whole mammoth family units were slaughtered at one time, it seems unlikely that it happened with any frequency given the difficulty of bringing down just one individual using Clovis technology. Their skill as hunters must have been extraordinary. Experimental attempts to penetrate the thick skin of recently deceased zoo elephants using Clovis weaponry have produced relatively unsatisfactory results except in areas of the rib cage behind the front leg and the abdominal area. Small targets indeed!

Since camel and horse remains have been found with those of mammoths and bison at many Clovis kill sites, some researchers believe that these animals also were Clovis prey. Detailed stratigraphic analyses at Lehner Ranch and Murray Springs, Arizona, and at Blackwater Draw, New Mexico, suggest that these animals were not abundant, possibly at the verge of extinction, before the advent of the Clovis hunters.

Evidence of possible horse butchery is seen at Murray Springs, Arizona, and at Midland, Lubbock Lake, and Bonfire Shelter, Texas. Smaller animals also are found occasionally, with indications that they, too, were part of the Clovis larder—tapir (*Tapirus* spp.) and black bear (*Ursus americanus*) at Lehner ranch and tapir, peccary (*Platygonus* sp.), and short-faced bear (*Arctodus* sp.) at Lubbock Lake. Even smaller creatures, such as turtles and turkeys, became part of the Clovis menu to judge from the evidence at Lubbock Lake, Texas.

Several Clovis bison kills are known—including Murray Springs, Arizona, where artifactual material remaining in the bone bed could be rejoined to discarded projectile points from the camp site. The camp was located nearly ten feet higher and 250 feet south of the kill site and butchering floor.

Skeleton and reconstruction of *Mylodon harlani* (Harlan's ground sloth). Photograph by Marc Gaede, from the MNA photo archives

Clovis tool inventories indicate the dominance of that New World invention, the Clovis fluted point. The Clovis flintknappers were master craftsmen who utilized the best raw materials to be found in a region. Many of their raw material sources are still unknown. In addition to the fluted points, they made composite tools from blades using thinning and shaping techniques. They also made tools from large stone flakes, bone, and ivory, and they fashioned mammoth bone shaft wrenches. Although there are very few clues to their social and religious customs, we have found a possible red-ochre burial site with an associated cache of lithic materials at the Anzick site in Montana. A newly discovered site, Richey-Roberts,

Above: "Moab Mastodon" petroglyph. Opposite right: Clovis point found in a canyon on the plateau. Photographs by Adrienne Anderson

which is near Winatchee, Washington, appears to be similar to the Anzick cache.

Clovis Chronology

In 1964, we had six radiocarbon-dated western sites in which Clovis artifacts had been found *in situ* with an average age of 11,260 years. New information corroborates this date and provides a very visible archaeochronologic marker for the Clovis in North America.

Geological and (in my opinion) archaeological evidence indicates that the Clovis people were the "explorers" who first penetrated and then populated an entire new hemisphere. Their exploration may have been accidental (caused by a rising sea level that flooded the Bering land bridge and left them stranded in the New World), or it may have been deliberate, a purposeful expansion of nomadic hunters in search of game or new hunting grounds. One may see it also as pure adventure, the human desire to "see what lies beyond the horizon." Whatever the case, it seems clear that Clovis hunters penetrated the temperate zones of North America and spread south in all directions.

Clovis People on the Colorado Plateau

Fluted projectile points designated as Clovis were not identified on the Colorado Plateau until 1959-60. The general scarcity of Paleo-Indian material from Utah and the Desert West in general (plus a lack of knowledge as to the abundance of their prey) led early investigators to assume that these cultural traditions were not present in this region. We now know that was not the case.

In the past decade, we have learned that extinct Pleistocene megafauna were common, if not abundant, on the Colorado Plateau. In 1985, I constructed a map of mammoth distribution, as it was then known, for the Southwest. Using what information was available, I constructed a similar map for the Clovis point distribution. Not surprisingly, there is a similarity in the distribution pattern of Clovis projectile points and the distribution of known mammoth sites. It appears that both mammoths and mammoth hunters frequented the well-watered portions of the Colorado Plateau, such as the Little Colorado, Colorado, San Juan, and Green rivers as well as their major tributaries.

Possible Clovis Petroglyphs

At least three examples of rock art from the plateau depict proboscideans, presumed to be mammoths. The best known of these occurs near Moab, Utah, and is generally called the "Moab Mastodon." There has been some doubt expressed over the years as to its authenticity; in addition, it reportedly has been "enhanced" by freshening the peck marks of the petroglyph. Even more unfortunately, the art has suffered recent damage from high-powered rifles.

Several other petroglyphs from the area also seem to be mammoth representations. Interestingly, they occur in a canyon that also has produced mammoth remains. It is my firm belief that people and mammoths (as well as other extinct fauna) were contemporaries on the Colorado Plateau.

Clovis People and Pleistocene Extinctions

A recent theory called "Pleistocene Overkill" postulates that human hunters advancing as a "wave" of predation exterminated the mammoth and other large Pleistocene lifeforms. Opponents of this theory suggest that climatic stress/floral community recombination is a more likely cause. Perhaps elements of both theories were factors in the Pleistocene megafauna extinction.

Folsom People

With the extinction (or extermination) of mammoths, evidence of the Clovis culture also disappeared. The next younger, most widespread artifact horizon that we find is known as the Folsom culture. It is defined by a smaller, more delicate fluted point called the Folsom point, which has a nearly one-hundred percent correlation with bison procurement.

Folsom points actually were the first fluted projectile points to be found and recognized as associated with Pleistocene fauna. The name comes from a bison bone bed in the banks of an arroyo near Folsom, New Mexico. Most anthropologists in the 1930s believed that humans had no greater antiquity in the New World than 3,000 years. Therefore, when a paleontological excavation crew from the Denver Museum of Natural History discovered fluted projectile points in uncontestable association with the bones of an extinct form of bison, it threw a shock wave through the North American archaeological community that is akin to the physical shock wave of the San Francisco earthquake of 1906 (or 1989). When another fluted projectile point (the Clovis point) was found with mammoth remains shortly thereafter, New World archaeological theory was in shambles.

The evidence of Folsom people is not as geographically widespread as it is for their Clovis predecessors. It does seem likely, however, that the Folsom culture was a "retooling" or modification of the Clovis technology after the depletion of the mammoth as a food source. Since the Folsom projectile point seems to be a smaller, more stylized version of the Clovis point, it might reflect an adaptation to a smaller, fleeter quarry—the bison.

The lifestyle of Folsom people, as reconstructed from the archaeological evidence, appears to be that of nomadic bison hunters, similar in many ways to their mammoth-hunting predecessors. Most sites and remains of Folsom people date back to approximately 10,000 years ago.

Folsom People on the Colorado Plateau

As with the Clovis culture, archaeologists know very little about the daily lives and customs of the Folsom people on the Colorado Plateau. Much of what we do know is derived from scattered surface finds of individual Folsom points collected since the mid-1950s. No sites containing multiple tools, tool types, and other evidence of camp activity were known from the Arizona portion of the Colorado Plateau until 1975. Not until 1984 did the Utah portion produce its first Folsom site.

When an approach similar to the one used to show coincidence of Clovis artifacts and mammoth sites is utilized to prepare a map of reported bison localities and Folsom artifacts on the Colorado Plateau, we see again a distributional coincidence of bison and bison hunters.

There is, however, a probable bias to the distribution map for bison. The map does not accurately represent bison range on the plateau. There are several reasons for this inaccuracy—including the paucity of literature citing bison remains and the inability of many observers to differentiate bison remains from those of modern cattle. An additional problem is that bison distribution is not restricted to the Pleistocene, as it was for mammoth, but includes Holocene localities as well. A chronology for bison remains on the Colorado Plateau (dated localities), though it would be very useful to researchers, is essentially nonexistent.

Plano Cultures

The youngest subdivision of the Lithic stage contains a variety of lanceolate, stemmed, and indented projectile points that reflect different geographical type localities. Names such as Alberta, Agate Basin, Eden Valley, Scottsbluff, Cody, and Plainview refer to projectile point types with different stylistic attributes and also are used to designate groups of people or cultures.

Most Plano cultures seem to have been bison hunters. While there is some evidence (in the form of scattered projectile points) that these groups lived and hunted on the Colorado Plateau, no one has yet plotted their distribution in detail or studied their chronological interval on the plateau. Ironically, we know even less about this cultural interval on the Colorado Plateau than we do about the two preceding cultures.

Pleistocene Big-Game Hunters

Archaeological publications before 1980 (and some since then!) have tended to eliminate the probability of Clovis, Folsom, and Plano cultural stages from the Colorado Plateau. The reason most often cited for the proposed absence is the assumed paucity of megafaunal (big-game) resources on the plateau. However, recent evidence does not seem to support such a conclusion. Using only mammoth and

"Big Game Hunter's Campsite." Acrylic painting by Denny Carley

bison as game animals and only Clovis through Plano cultural stages as hunters, we are able to create distribution maps that lead to some very interesting conclusions: first, there appears to have been a relative abundance of mammoth on the Colorado Plateau during the late Pleistocene and of bison during the late Pleistocene and early Holocene. Moreover, evidence of the existence of early cultural entities such as the Clovis on the plateau is also relatively abundant. Only one other geographical region in the United States produces as great an indication of the presence of both hunters and hunted at these early intervals of North American prehistory. That region is the High Plains region of New Mexico, Texas, and Oklahoma.

The presence of both mammoth and bison has been documented in the very heart of the Colorado Plateau—to within 700 years of the extinction of mammoths. This is contemporaneous with the best evidence of the earliest human culture on the plateau. Does this imply that humans exterminated the Pleistocene megafauna of the region, as postulated by the "overkill" hypothesis? Or, does it indicate a human "coup de grace" to a population already in climatic or dietary stress? These questions and others are what make the late Pleistocene and early Holocene research so exciting.

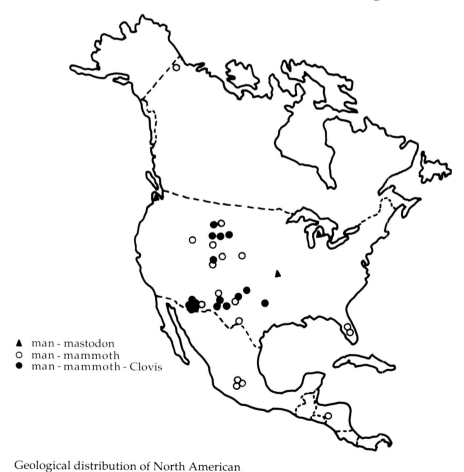

▲ man - mastodon
○ man - mammoth
● man - mammoth - Clovis

Geological distribution of North American
man and mammoth/mastodon sites.
Illustration by Larry Agenbroad

HUNTERS AND GATHERERS: THE ARCHAIC PEOPLES

Archaic Peoples

Archaeologists most often use the term "Archaic stage" to refer to prehistoric people with a migratory hunting-and-gathering lifestyle. The particular timeframe assigned to this cultural stage varies with location and group. For the Colorado Plateau, the Archaic stage occupies the period of approximately 2,000 to 8,500 years ago. In some areas, it may have lasted until contact with European cultures! The Archaic fills the temporal and cultural gap between the big-game (mammoth and bison) hunters and the later sedentary or semi-sedentary horticulturalists and agriculturalists dependent on a corn-bean-squash resource base.

Archaic Cultural Traits

With the Archaic peoples, we gain several new "dimensions" of artifacts. For example, the use of vegetable materials for clothing, cordage, basketry, etc. is fairly common among Archaic peoples. It is virtually unknown in the earlier cultural manifestations on the Colorado Plateau. In addition to these items, grinding stones (manos and metates) are nearly omnipresent. Metates are often "slab" or "basin" types, while the most common manos are "cobble" (or one-hand) manos.

Sandal of the Archaic people. Photograph by Larry Agenbroad

Opposite, bottom; above; and right:
Petroglyphs found at Newspaper
Rock near Monticello, Utah.
Photographs by Larry Agenbroad

Split-twig figurine. Illustration
after S. M. Wheeler (1942)

Another new dimension is art. Barrier Canyon-style pictographs (Archaic in age) are probably the earliest pictograph style known in Utah. Just as intriguing as the Barrier Canyon pictographs is a second artistic trait associated with the Colorado Plateau Archaic—the split-twig figurines. These animal representations appear to have magico-religious purpose in their earliest context; some of the figurines are even neatly pierced with miniature spears. They apparently became less ritualistic, and more common, in the late Archaic. A series of radiocarbon dates places these items between 3,100 and 4,100 years ago. Is it possible the altithermal drought caused such resource stress that Archaic people tried to invoke supernatural aid through offerings of split-twig figurines? From what we know of the physical evidence of environmental change in the mid-Holocene, such a theory is plausible.

ENVIRONMENTAL CHANGE

At this point, we should pause to consider the events that would shift cultural focus from hunting, as in the preceding Llano and Plano stages, to a hunting-and-gathering lifeway.

There is increasing evidence of rather dramatic change in the climate of the Colorado Plateau area through the Holocene. In the 1940s, geologists used this information to produce a geoclimatic model that has been championed *and* vilified by later researchers. Most facets of the geoclimatic dating model for the western portions of North America (including the Colorado Plateau) appear to be correct. Researchers studying Holocene and Pleistocene alluvial (stream-laid) deposits find cycles of erosion and deposition recorded in the banks of modern arroyo walls, such as Tsegi Canyon and nearby drainages.

Recent studies using a powerful new technique, radiocarbon dating, generally substantiate older relative dating models. For instance, although it is still being debated, it appears that the altithermal drought was a reality. It may have varied with latitude, elevation, or local conditions, but much of the arid and semiarid West was even more arid during the interval of 4,500 to 7,500 years ago. Since increased aridity means decreased vegetation and, thus, a greatly reduced fauna, the primary food resource of the big-game hunting cultural groups disappeared. Successful human responses to such environmental stress would include migration to more favorable habitat or the increased exploitation and utilization of new resources—vegetable resources. Hence, the Archaic cultural groups.

We know more about the Archaic peoples on the northern Colorado Plateau than we do about those residing on the southern Colorado Plateau because they have been studied more thoroughly. It appears that there are two somewhat different aspects of the Archaic on the plateau. The approximate boundary for these subdivisions is a natural one—the Colorado River. However, in the Cataract Canyon portion of the Colorado River, Archaic sites and pictograph panels indicative of the same cultural entity occur on both sides of the river, which suggests that the Colorado River was not an impenetrable barrier to Archaic people.

The archaeological "visibility" of pre-ceramic cultures on the Colorado Plateau provides us with some information on their travel routes into the area. Clovis hunters appear to have entered the plateau from the Rio Grande region via the Puerco and Little Colorado river systems—or from the Green River region of Wyoming via the Green, Colorado, and Yampa river drainages with an indication of some movement from the northern Great Basin. Folsom and Plano patterns are nearly the same as Clovis. Archaic cultures appear to have used the Great Basin routes, the lower Grand Canyon, and the southwestern desert (Basin and Range) as additional avenues of access to the plateau.

When looking at the distribution map for Archaic sites on the Colorado Plateau, realize that this represents only a small portion of the number of known locations. The map represents the geographical scatter, not the individual sites. Contrasted to the preceding Lithic stage, the number of localities is staggering. Archaeological "visibility" is much better for the Archaic than for the preceding Plano and Llano stages. With this greater visibility, with stratified sites (sites with many layers of artifacts), and with increased chronological control, the Archaic is still (in essence) an archaeological "no-man's land." Why?

By analogy, attempting to interpret the archaeological prehistory of the Colorado Plateau (11,000 years) from the perspective of Anasazi prehistory (2,000 years) is like trying to interpret the history of the United States since its "discovery" by Columbus (500 years) by what is known of events that have transpired since A.D. 1900 (90 years). In both cases, most of the information is missing. And in both

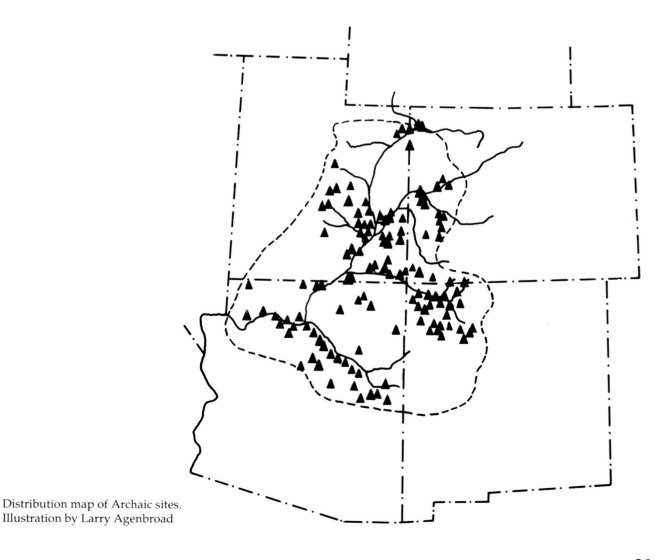

Distribution map of Archaic sites.
Illustration by Larry Agenbroad

cases, using only the most recent twenty percent of history means that the majority of the intrigue, adventure, and romance is lost.

In my opinion, archaeologists have overemphasized the most recent prehistory of the Colorado Plateau. I would estimate that more than ninety percent of our archaeological effort has been expended on the Anasazi and other Formative groups. This means that there are 9,000 years (at least) of prehistoric cultural remains out there—waiting to give us insight into all of the Colorado Plateau's prehistory. Think about it for a few minutes. There were groups of people coexisting with and exploiting at least part of a large faunal resource of now-extinct Pleistocene animals. What was it like to live on the Colorado Plateau in the terminal phases of the Pleistocene? How did these people adapt to a major loss of their animal resource base? We know that they did because their archaeological "visibility" is there even though it is not well seen or understood. What adaptations did these people make later, during what may be described as an "environmental crash?"

The real dynamics of prehistoric cultural adaptation to the Colorado Plateau environment lie, barely noticed, hardly understood, in that 9,000 year interval. In my opinion, we need to develop something analogous to polaroid sunglasses—glasses that will allow field archaeologists to "filter out" the ceramic cultures and focus on the less abundant and more difficult to interpret remains of Archaic and Lithic groups.

Left: Exploitation of the lacustrine environment of Pleistocene lakes that are now dry.
Above: "Desert Subsistence."
Acrylic paintings by Denny Carley

As a final statement, the Paleo-Indian period of the Colorado Plateau, as we presently know it, is derived from the efforts of a large number of individuals. A substantial amount of artifacts have been recovered by the nonprofessional (i.e., avocational archaeologist) public. Private collections from the area contain a large body of information—a great deal of which has not been called to the attention of professional researchers. This statement is as true for paleontological resources as it is for archaeological resources. I would like to encourage these people to make their collections and localities known so that the material can be photographed and measured and the geographical locality plotted. Cooperation and mutual respect between the professional and amateur communities is one of the most important keys to unlocking the secrets of the aceramic prehistory—the record of the Paleo-Indians on the Colorado Plateau.

31

ABOUT THE AUTHOR

Dr. Larry D. Agenbroad is a professor of geology and director of the Quaternary Studies Program at Northern Arizona University. His degrees include a B.S. in Geological Engineering, a M.S. in Economic Geology, a M.A. in Anthropology (Archaeology), and a Ph.D. in Hydrogeology—all from the University of Arizona, Tucson. His current research interests include Quaternary geology, geochronolgy, paleontology (Pleistocene megafauna), paleoecology, paleoclimatology, and pre-ceramic prehistory of the Colorado Plateau.

SUGGESTED READING

Cordell, Linda
1984 *Prehistory of the Southwest* (Orlando: Academic Press).

Fagan, Brian
1987 *The Great Journey: The Peopling of Ancient America* (London: Thames and Hudson Ltd.).

Jennings, Jesse
1964 *Prehistoric Man in the New World* (Chicago: University of Chicago Press).

1968 *Prehistory of North America* (New York: McGraw-Hill).

1978 *Prehistory of Utah and the Eastern Great Basin* (University of Utah Anthropological Papers No. 98).

1980 *Cowboy Cave* (University of Utah Anthropological Papers No. 104).

Martin, P.S. and R.G. Klein (eds.)
1984 *Quaternary Extinctions: A Prehistoric Revolution* (Tucson: University of Arizona Press).

West, Frederick H.
1981 *The Archaeology of Beringia* (New York: Columbia University Press).

Wheeler, S. M.
1942   *Archeology of Etna Cave, Lincoln County, Nevada* (Carson City: Nevada State Park Commission).

Plateau Managing Editor: Diana Clark Lubick
Graphic Design by Dianne Moen Zahnle
Color Separations by American Color
Typography by MacTypeNet
Printing by Land O'Sun Printers